MAKE YOUR OWN
BEADS
AND
JEWELRY

AN ILLUSTRATED,
STEP–BY–STEP GUIDE

JEWELRY DESIGNERS

Marie LeFevre
Michele's Designs
The Beadery

CONTRIBUTING WRITER/CONSULTANT

Karen Stolzenberg

Publications International, Ltd.

Marie LeFevre, of Crafts End Design Studio, is a teacher, designer, demonstrator, and consultant to the crafts industry. She has authored many books, including several on the subjects of paper and beaded jewelry. She is a member of the Society of Craft Designers and the Decorative Art Society. Her jewelry designs appear at pages 8, 14, 38, 41, 45, 47, 52, 54, 56, 58, and 60.

Michele J. Emerson-Roberts, of Michele's Designs, is a designer whose work has been published in a variety of magazines. Her many skills include making jewelry and wearable arts and decorative painting. She is a member of the Society of Craft Designers and the National Society of Decorative Painters. Her jewelry designs appear at pages 23, 26, 27, 30, 33, 36, 43, 50, and 62.

Karen Stolzenberg is a jewelry maker and fiber artist whose work combines her interest in textiles and beading. She is a high school art teacher and also teaches at the Art Institute of Chicago, where she combines an extensive background in multicultural art with diverse technical skills. Her jewelry design appears at page 11.

Special thanks to The Beadery, which provided assorted beads, faceted stones, cabochons, and stone holders used in this book. The Beadery's jewelry designs appear at pages 16, 18, and 20.

Photography
Sacco Productions Limited/Chicago

Photographers
Chris Brooks, Tom O'Connell, and Peter Ross

Photo Stylist
Melissa J. Sacco

Models
Karen Blaschek and Theresa Lesniak/Royal Model Management

Following are manufacturers whose products are used in this book: American Art Clay Co., Inc., 4717 W. 16th St., Indianapolis, IN 46222; The Beadery Craft Products, P.O. Box 178, Hope Valley, RI 02832; Bond Adhesives Co., 301 Frelinghuysen Ave., Newark, NJ 07114; DecoArt, P.O. Box 360, Stanford, KY 40484; Delta Technical Coatings, 2550 Pellissier Place, Whittier, CA 90601; Eberhardt-Faber, 8430 Neumarkt, Germany (a U.S. distributor for FIMO polymer clay is American Art Clay Co., Inc.); Madeira Marketing Ltd., 600 E. 9th St., Michigan City, IN 46360; Therm O Web, 770 Glenn Ave., Wheeling, IL 60090; and Tulip Productions, 24 Prime Pkwy., Natick, MA 01760.

CONTENTS

INTRODUCTION

One of the most personal ways of expressing ourselves is through what we wear—our choice of clothing and accessories helps us create the image we desire.

Among the earliest forms of human adornment were beads and jewelry. Whether they were meant to attract a mate, ward off evil spirits, or show social status, beads and jewelry offered ways to explore style and make a personal statement. Today, we still value beautiful beadwork. And though we may use beads and jewelry less for social or religious purposes than for their fashion appeal, we are blessed with virtually unlimited choices and supplies. Whether the beads are old, new, glass, ceramic, bone, gem stone, or plastic, jewelry designers need only use their imagination to create one-of-a-kind pieces.

In this book, we show various jewelry-making processes in step-by-step fashion. Because there are new "friendly" materials available, even the beginning jewelry artist can create pieces that are simple, inexpensive, professional looking—and fun to make. We also give you information about tools and materials and some of the techniques that will help you complete the projects in this book.

Maybe you've never strung a necklace in your life or made a quick repair to a jewelry clasp with your household pliers. Even so, this book will quickly teach you how to make beautiful jewelry to wear or give as gifts—and at a *fraction* of what you'd pay for comparable items in the stores!

BASIC SUPPLIES

Here are some supplies you will need in order to get started.

Needlenose Pliers and Wire Cutter. There are various kinds of

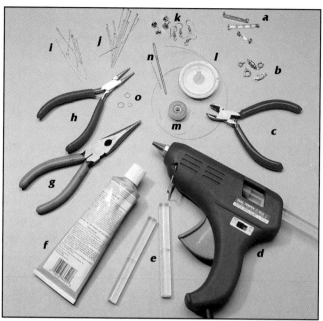

Jewelry-making supplies: a) pin backs; b) clasps; c) wire cutter; d) glue gun; e) glue sticks; f) jewelry glue; g) needlenose pliers/wire cutter; h) needlenose pliers; i) eye pins; j) head pins; k) earring backs and hooks; l) tigertail; m) beading thread; n) beading needles; o) jump rings.

pliers on the market. Select a pair that has a small, tapered head. Some have rounded points with a spring action, which can be useful in attaching head pins. It wouldn't hurt to have a couple pairs of needlenose pliers on hand: The shape of the snout varies, and different snouts work best for different techniques.

A wire cutter is a must for jewelry making, since you will be working with wire of varying thicknesses. You might consider getting a needlenose pliers with a built-in wire cutter—it's handy and may be cheaper than buying two different tools.

Beading Needles. Beading needles come in a wide range of sizes and types. It is best to purchase some that are intended for fine work and others that are larger. A variety of tapestry needles is also a good investment. These can be used for stringing larger beads and

making holes in polymer clay beads.

Beading Threads and Wires. Various materials can be used to string beads, and most hobby and craft stores or fabric shops will carry them. Nylon beading thread is flexible and strong. It can be used to string smaller beads. Waxed linen, which is very strong and durable, is useful in stringing large beads.

Neither nylon nor waxed linen should be used to string metal beads, since the metal edges will eventually wear through the thread and break it. Wire—the recommended material—comes in a variety of gauges; the lower the gauge number, the greater the thickness. There is also a beading thread called tigertail. This is a metal wire, and, because of its durability, it is perfect for stringing metal beads. Another possibility is rattail, a fabric thread that comes in an assortment of thicknesses and colors.

Glues and Gluing. There are many glues on the market. Choose those that are made especially for jewelry. They should be strong glues, providing a durable bond. Glue guns are sometimes preferred, depending on the project.

Findings. Findings are the small parts needed to put your projects together. They include head pins, eye pins, earring backs, pin backs, stickpin clutches, jump rings, and necklace clasps.

Beads. Most beads, stones, and stone holders (used for earrings and button covers) that we will be using in our projects are readily available from hobby or craft stores. There are many other sources for beads, however. With the revived interest in beadwork, specialty stores have sprung up everywhere. You can also recycle beads from clothing bought at garage sales or in thrift shops.

Polymer Clay. Polymer clay has been on the market for some time. It offers a wonderful and inexpensive way to design and make your own beads.

Miscellaneous Supplies. Most of the other supplies that are needed—scissors, waxed paper, plastic wrap, poster board, etc.— can be obtained from hobby or craft shops or from local grocery or hardware stores.

TECHNIQUES

Gluing. Gluing needs to be done neatly and carefully. Use tiny amounts of glue: Nothing will spoil the prettiest jewelry quite like an unsightly glob of glue. One way to ensure that you use only small amounts is to apply the glue with a toothpick. Put a small dab of glue on the toothpick and then apply exactly where you want the glue to go. Be sure to wipe away any excess.

Applying Polymer and Varnish Finishes. Neatness is again the name of the game. Be sure to use clean brushes and apply in thin,

even coats. It is much better to apply a second coat than to put on a heavy first coat that will dry unevenly or—worse—drip.

Making Knots. A number of knots are used in jewelry making.

To make a **slip knot,** make a circle or loop in one end of your thread, with the short tail (B) passing underneath the remaining length of the thread (A).

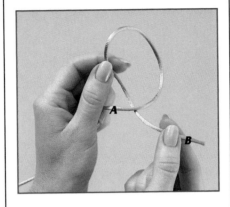

A short distance from the loop, make a second loop in end A.

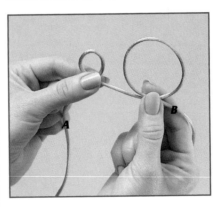

Pass the second loop, from behind, through the first loop.

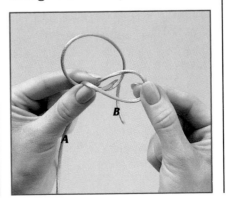

As you hold the second loop, pull end B down and tight.

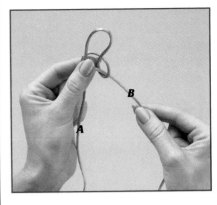

You should have created a knot that can get larger or smaller by sliding the long tail up or down.

To make an overhand knot, create a loop with your string (note A and B).

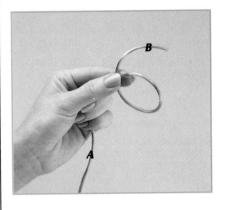

Pass end B around and through the loop from behind.

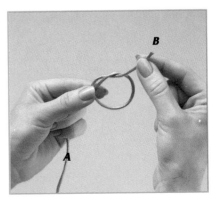

Pull tight.

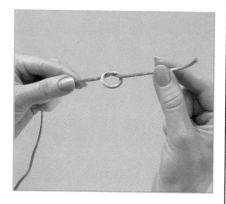

Polymer Clays. There are several polymer clays on the market. All are intermixable and offer you endless options for creating beads.

The clays are quite hard when first unwrapped and must be kneaded until soft and pliable. Make sure not to use the clay before it reaches this stage—if you do, you may create air pockets and cracks when you roll it out, and this can cause the clay to break apart.

Most beads begin as long logs fashioned by combining several smaller logs, rolling them together, then cutting them into small pieces.

This technique can also be used to create beads with intricate designs. By placing small pieces of clay on the surface of a bead being formed, then rolling the bead, you can create novel, one-of-a-kind designs.

After forming your beads, put holes in them before baking. This can be done with a needle, a ceramicist's needle tool, a toothpick, or a wire (such as a piece of floral stem wire).

When perforating a bead, hold it gently, then carefully drill through the bead, smoothing both ends when finished. Be sure that your hole is large enough to accommodate the thread you will be using. Bake your beads for about 30 minutes at 265 degrees Fahrenheit.

After the clay is baked, you can either leave the matte surface undisturbed or varnish it. Some brands of polymer clay make a varnish for applying a gloss finish.

Plastic Modeling **Material.** This material is available in a wide range of colors and metallic finishes and comes in sheets, smaller flat pieces, and pellets.

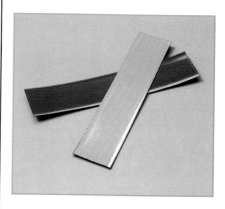

It needs to be heated until soft and pliable; this is most easily done by immersing in water heated to between 140 and 150 degrees Fahrenheit. Use a heat-resistant, nonaluminum bowl.

When the plastic is soft enough, you can shape it any way you wish; you can also put it into molds to give it a predetermined shape. Each time you need to change the shape as you work on the piece, just rewarm it in the water.

The plastic can be cut when it just starts to harden.

Heat-bonding Material. It is best to fuse the heat-bonding material to your fabric before you cut it, since making sure that all edges are fused—especially with smaller pieces of fabric, like ribbon—can otherwise be difficult.

Place the heat-bonding material on the wrong side of your fabric; leave the paper backing of the heat-bonding material undisturbed.

Put your iron on the heat setting specified in the manufacturer's directions. Apply the iron to the area or areas to be fused, checking periodically. After bonding has occurred, let the fabric cool.

Cut out the pieces; leave the paper side of the heat-bonding material intact until you are ready to adhere the fabric to another surface, such as poster board or cloth.

Head Pins. Working with head pins can be a little awkward at first, but once you have learned to use your needlenose pliers, it will become a smooth operation.

Head pins, which resemble large straight pins with a flat head, come in different lengths. Using the longest size allows for more flexibility when determining the correct length, based on the number and sizes of beads you will be stringing.

Begin by inserting the head pin into the bead hole—the bead will sit securely on the flat end of the pin.

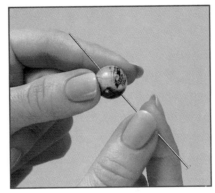

Determine the length you need to make your "eye," or closure, which will attach to a necklace wire, an earring hook, or the like. It should be about $1/4$ inch. Then, with a wire cutter or the cutter part of the pliers, snip off the rest of the head pin.

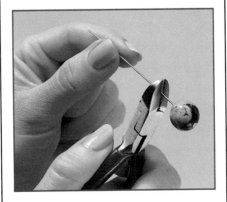

Grip the exposed length of wire with your pliers and gently twist the wire around to form a circle that closes as near as possible to the top of the bead. You have now formed an eye that can be used in stringing.

Eye Pins. Eye pins also come in different lengths, but instead of having a flat bottom, they have an eye, or circle, at the end. This allows for hanging things from the pin or for linking units together, as in a bracelet.

Treat an eye pin much as you would a head pin—that is, string on your beads and allow about $1/4$ inch of wire above the top bead to form the eye pin's closure. Using a needlenose pliers, carefully twist the wire to form the circle as close as you can to the top of the bead.

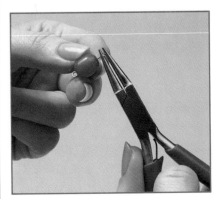

KARMA

CLAY BEAD NECKLACE

The mystique of India inspired this clay-bead-and-stone creation, enhanced by a silver-washed buddha bead at its center. It will add interest to the most basic dress, blouse, or sweater. The necklace makes an especially handsome complement to casual attire, dressing it up without overwhelming.

1 Package Each of White and Black Polymer Clay (we used FIMO polymer clay)

Ruler

Rolling Pin

Single-edged Razor Blade

2 Floral Stem Wires

Baking Pan

Beading Needle

White Beading Thread

3 2mm Round Black Beads

5 Turquoise Spacer Beads

1 Silver-washed Buddha Bead

4 Coral Barrel Beads

4 Round Turquoise Beads

4 Antiqued Silver Pony Beads

2 White Barrel Beads

2 Oval Amber Beads

12-inch Silver Chain

Scissors

CAUTION: When using FIMO, do not bake above 265 degrees Fahrenheit, and use a separate thermometer to verify actual oven temperature. Do not overbake, as fumes could be toxic. If you lengthen the baking time, lower the temperature to 250 degrees. Do not swallow FIMO, and supervise children at all times when baking. Never use a pan or sheet in food preparation that you have used previously to bake FIMO.

☉ ☉ ☉ ☉ ☉ ☉

MAKING THE BEADS
See also "Techniques" section of Introduction.

1. Prepare the packages of white and black polymer clay by kneading them. Divide each color in half.

2. You will need to make marbled clay for this project. To do this, roll one of the black halves and one of the white halves by hand, using the ruler to measure two 6-inch lengths. Combine the rolls of white and black clay, twisting them together until they are marbled. Don't overwork the clay, or the colors will blend.

3. You will also need to make jelly roll portions for the beads. To do this, take the remaining two halves of white and black clay and, with the rolling pin, roll them into two sheets, each measuring 4 inches square. Put one sheet on top of the other, then roll up the combined sheets tightly. Using the single-edged razor blade, cut off a ³/₄-inch length from the jelly roll log.

4. With the rolling pin, flatten one-quarter of the marbled clay roll into a 2-inch-square piece.

5. To make the spiral clay bead just above the buddha bead, use the razor blade to cut a rectangle, measuring 1³/₄ inches by ³/₄ inch, from the marbled sheet. Place the ³/₄-inch length of jelly roll on the rectangle and wrap the marbled clay around the jelly roll core. Gently roll to join the clays smoothly.

6. To make the two oblong clay beads, cut four ¹/₈-inch pieces from the jelly roll log. Take the remaining marbled clay roll and, using the flat of your hand, roll it into a ¹/₈-inch-diameter log. Cut this in thirds and set aside one of the thirds (you will use it later to make the final round clay bead). Take two of the ¹/₈-inch jelly roll pieces and wrap one marbled log around them so that their jelly roll design will show on opposite sides of the bead. Roll into a 1-inch cylinder. Repeat for the second oblong clay bead.

7. For the round clay bead, cut off two more 1/8-inch pieces from the jelly roll log with the razor blade. Using the remaining third of the marbled log that you set aside earlier, repeat the instructions above for the oblong clay bead, but roll the clay into a round, instead of cylindrical, bead.

8. Pierce the clay bead centers with the floral stem wires. Place the wires across the baking pan and bake for 30 minutes at 265 degrees Fahrenheit. Let the beads cool.

STRINGING THE NECKLACE

1. Thread the beading needle with the white beading thread. Tie a double overhand knot at one end of the thread (see discussion of knots in "Techniques" section of Introduction). String on one 2mm round black bead, one turquoise spacer bead, one 2mm round black bead, the round clay bead, one 2mm round black bead, the silver-washed buddha bead, the spiral clay bead.

2. Continue with one coral barrel bead, one turquoise spacer bead, one round turquoise bead, one oblong clay bead, one antiqued silver pony bead, one coral barrel bead, one antiqued silver pony bead, one round turquoise bead, one turquoise spacer bead, one white barrel bead, one oval amber bead.

3. String through one end of the silver chain, threading down through the beads to the coral bead above the spiral clay bead.

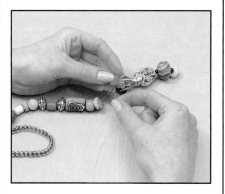

4. String through the coral barrel bead.

5. Start a new string of beads, repeating the pattern in step 2.

6. String through the other end of the chain, then bring the thread back down through the beads.

7. Continue threading down through the beads. After you thread through the original 2mm round black bead, knot the thread and trim the excess with the scissors.

DECO

CLAY BEAD NECKLACE

Each bead in this fabulous necklace seems to tell a little story, interweaving gray, black, and white designs in a harmonious—and unique—whole. Though it looks complicated, the piece is almost a snap: The secret is how you roll the clay. You'll pick up the technique with ease!

2 Packages Each of Gray, Black, and White Polymer Clay (we used FIMO polymer clay)

Single-edged Razor Blade

Tapestry Needle

1 Package of Floral Stem Wires

Baking Pan

40 Toothpicks

Polymer Clay Varnish

Varnish Brush

Foamcore Board (typically used to back framed prints)

Silver-tone Necklace Clasp

Gray or Black Waxed Linen

Beading Needle

Scissors

CAUTION: When using FIMO, do not bake above 265 degrees Fahrenheit, and use a separate thermometer to verify actual oven temperature. Do not overbake, as fumes could be toxic. If you lengthen the baking time, lower the temperature to 250 degrees. Do not swallow FIMO, and supervise children at all times when baking. Never use a pan or sheet in food preparation that you have used previously to bake FIMO.

⊙　⊙　⊙　⊙　⊙　⊙

MAKING THE BEADS
See also "Techniques" section of Introduction.

1. Knead each package of polymer clay separately until it is soft and pliable.

2. Take the two packages of gray polymer clay, combine them, and roll into a log about 3/4 inch in diameter and 14 to 16 inches long. Take the two packages of black polymer clay, combine them, and roll into a long rod about 1/8 inch to 1/4 inch in diameter; do the same with the two packages of white polymer clay. With the single-edged razor blade, cut off three 14- to 16-inch lengths from both the black rod and the white rod. Position the thin rods lengthwise on the gray log, alternating colors and spacing evenly.

3. Roll the log until the surface is smooth and the length 20 inches. With the razor blade, cut off a 1/2-inch piece to make the first bead. Cut the rest of the log in pieces of equal length. You should have a total of 40 pieces of cut log.

4. Roll the first piece of cut log into a thin snake 4 to 5 inches long. Try to keep the stripes from twisting.

Join the ends and form a circle, then shape the circle into an equal-sided triangle.

5. Lay a finger lightly across two corners and one side of the triangle to hold it down. Lift another side and, using your thumb and fore-finger, roll the striped clay toward the center so that the striping twists. Now, do the same for the other two sides of the triangle.

Form a Y shape by pushing the midpoints of the triangle sides together (toward what used to be the center of the triangle) and pinching them.

6. Bring the three sides of the Y up together and carefully join them. Roll gently to form the bead.

7. Take the remaining white and black rods; twist and spiral them together.

8. Roll the twist until it is smooth and a candy cane pattern results. The twist should measure about 1/8 inch in diameter and be 40 inches long. With the razor blade, cut 1-inch pieces from the twist.

9. Wrap a 1-inch length of the candy cane rod around your bead. Roll the bead until the candy cane design is fully integrated and the surface of the bead is smooth.

Repeat steps 4 through 9 to make the remaining 39 beads.

10. Pierce each bead carefully with the tapestry needle. smoothing the hole at both entry and exit. String the beads through the pieces of floral stem wire, spacing them well apart, and place the wires across the baking pan. Bake at 265 degrees Fahrenheit for 30 minutes. Let the beads cool before varnishing.

11. To varnish the beads, stick each bead on a toothpick and carefully apply the polymer clay varnish in a thin, even coat, using the varnish brush. Push the other end of the toothpick into the foamcore board and let dry.

STRINGING THE NECKLACE

1. Attach one end of the silver-tone necklace clasp to the waxed linen, tying a small overhand knot and leaving about a 2-inch tail of linen (see discussion of knots in "Techniques" section of Introduction).

2. String your beads (no needle is necessary) and attach the other end of the necklace clasp to the linen, tying a small overhand knot as close as possible to the clasp, but leaving a small space between the clasp and the last bead for flexibility.

3. After tying the knot at the clasp, leave about a 2-inch tail of linen. Thread the beading needle onto this tail and thread back through four beads; trim the remaining tail with the scissors. Repeat this to hide the linen tail at the other end of the necklace.

BABYLON

SILVER-AND-AMETHYST NECKLACE

The art of the ancient Middle East inspired this lovely arrangement of silver beads, amethyst chips, and purple discs. As the terra cotta variation suggests, the pattern can be used, again and again, with different sizes and styles of beads. Let your creativity be your guide!

MATERIALS

Beading Towel or Beading Board

Nylon Beading Thread

Silver-tone Necklace Clasp

Toothpick

Jewelry Glue

Scissors

23 Amethyst Bead Chips

20 Assorted Ornamental Silver-washed and Antiqued Silver Beads

9 1-inch Purple Spacer Discs

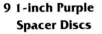

1. Lay out your bead design on the beading towel or beading board.

2. Put one end of the nylon beading thread through one ring of the silver-tone necklace clasp.

3. Tie an overhand knot (see discussion of knots in "Techniques"

section of Introduction). Using the toothpick, place a small amount of jewelry glue on top of the knot to hold it. With the scissors, trim the excess thread.

4. String your beads according to the pattern shown in step 1. At the center of the necklace should be three purple spacer discs.

5. Thread through the other end of the necklace clasp. Tie an overhand knot and secure it with a drop of jewelry glue applied with the toothpick. Trim the excess thread.

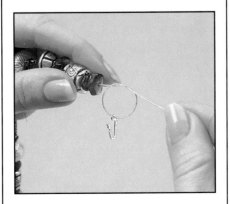

VARIATION

Using similar old-world-style pony beads in silver or gold, plus terra cotta beads, you can create an entirely new look using the same bead order. Or, vary the pattern, add beads to the design for a longer necklace . . . be as creative as you wish!

TIGRIS

SILVER-AND-GOLD NECKLACE

The unusual combination of antiqued silver and gold achieves a kind of harmony, while overhand knots in the black cord serve as a counterpoint to the metal beads, in this simple but elegant necklace reminiscent of ancient beadcraft.

MATERIALS

Scissors

4-yard Length of Black Rattail Cord

18 8mm Silver-washed Rings

6 10mm Antiqued Gold Melon Beads

5 Ornamental Antiqued Silver Pony Beads (two separate designs, with 2 matching beads and another different set of 3 matching beads)

4 Corrugated Antiqued Gold Discs

4 Corrugated Antiqued Silver Discs

4 Ornamental Antiqued Gold Pony Beads (two different matching pairs)

◉ ◉ ◉ ◉ ◉ ◉

Order of beads in necklace

1. With the scissors, cut three pieces of black rattail cord, each 46 inches long. Tie an overhand knot in each piece 18 inches from the end (see discussion of knots in "Techniques" section of Introduction).

2. Onto the long end of one of the rattail cord pieces, string beads for the first of the three short central strands: three silver-washed rings, one antiqued gold melon bead, one ornamental antiqued silver pony bead, one antiqued gold melon bead, three silver-washed rings. Slide them down to the knot. Tie a second knot 5 inches away from the first.

Repeat with the remaining two pieces of rattail cord. Make the second set of knots 6 inches apart and the last set 7 inches apart.

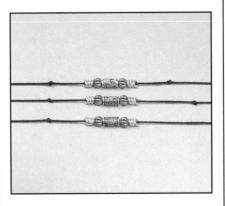

3. Hold the three strands of rattail cord so that the knots on one side of the center beads are even. String beads for one side of the necklace onto the three rattail cords held together, in the following order (see also photo showing order of beads), making overhand knots where indicated: one corrugated antiqued gold disc, one ornamental antiqued silver pony bead, one corrugated antiqued gold disc, one knot, one corrugated antiqued silver disc, one ornamental antiqued gold pony bead, one corrugated antiqued silver disc, one knot, one ornamental antiqued gold pony bead, one knot. Repeat for the other side of the necklace.

4. Tie all the rattail cords together at the back of the necklace, adjusting it to fit. Trim the ends with the scissors.

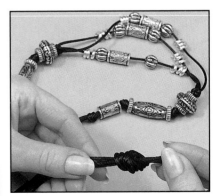

17

EUPHRATES

TWIN BEADED BRACELETS AND EARRINGS

Stretch cord is the secret to this comfortable double bracelet—and, because of the way the piece is constructed, you never have to worry about losing one of the circlets. Matching earrings complete this charming and versatile ensemble.

MAKING THE BRACELETS

M A T E R I A L S

- **20-inch Length of Black Stretch Cord**
- **8 Antiqued Silver Pony Beads (1 pair in each of 4 styles)**
- **20 Corrugated Terra Cotta Discs**
- **20 Corrugated Antiqued Silver Discs**
- **10 10mm Terra Cotta Melon Beads**
- **4 Heart-shaped Silver-washed Pony Beads**

⊙ ⊙ ⊙ ⊙ ⊙ ⊙

Order of beads in first circlet, from left to right, on beading board

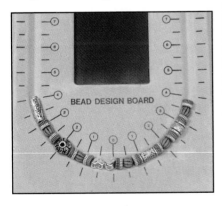

I. Make a large slip knot near the end of the black stretch cord to hold the beads (see discussion of knots in "Techniques" section of Introduction).

2. String on the beads for the first circlet of the twin bracelets, in the order shown on the beading board.

3. Thread the cord through the first bead a second time.

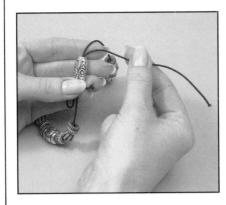

4. String on the mate to the first bead, then string on the same beads as in step 2, *but in reverse order*, beginning with a corrugated terra cotta disc (omit the first antiqued silver pony bead, since you've already strung it at the beginning of this step). Tie a slip knot at the end of the beads.

5. Undo the first slip knot you made and thread the stretch cord through the mate to the first bead.

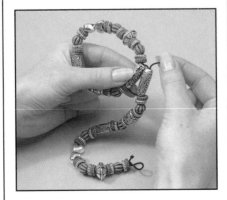

6. Undo the second slip knot. Holding both ends of the stretch cord, pull the beads together snugly and tie the ends of the cord in a single or double overhand knot close to the beads (see discussion of knots in "Techniques" section of Introduction). Hide the knot inside the mate to the first bead.

MAKING THE EARRINGS

M A T E R I A L S

- **2 1¹/₂-inch Silver-tone Head Pins**
- **4 6mm Silver-washed Rondelles**
- **4 10.5mm Corrugated Terra Cotta Discs**
- **2 Matching Antiqued Silver Pony Beads (identical to 1 pair in twin bracelets)**
- **2 4mm Round Black Beads**
- **Tweezers**
- **Silver-tone Earring Hooks**
- **Needlenose Pliers**

⊙ ⊙ ⊙ ⊙ ⊙ ⊙

I. String the beads onto a silver-tone head pin as follows: one 6mm silver-washed rondelle, one 10.5mm corrugated terra cotta disc, one antiqued silver pony bead, one 10.5mm corrugated terra cotta disc, one 6mm silver-washed rondelle, one 4mm round black bead. Use the tweezers to place the small black bead.

2. Thread the end of the head pin through the loop of a silver-tone earring hook. With the pliers, bend the pin into a closed loop. Repeat for the second earring.

M I D N I G H T

SAPPHIRE-LOOK BARRETTE AND EARRINGS

Deep-sapphire acrylic stones lend drama and interest to this barrette-and-earring duo. Reminiscent of the American Southwest in its design, yet urbane in its choice of cabochon colors, Midnight is a striking ensemble you'll delight in wearing, whatever the occasion.

MATERIALS

Scissors

26-inch Length of Black Rattail Cord

Jewelry Glue

1 3-inch Silver-tone Barrette

4-inch Length of $^3/_8$-inch Black Satin Ribbon

 8 10mm Antiqued Silver Melon Beads

 10 10.5mm Corrugated Antiqued Silver Discs

 3 9 × 6mm Barrel-shaped Black Pony Beads

 2 9 × 6mm Barrel-shaped Sapphire Pony Beads

 2 18 × 13mm Oval Silver Stone Holders

3 18mm Round Silver Stone Holders

 2 18 × 13mm Oval Faceted Acrylic Sapphire Stones

1 18mm Round Acrylic Sapphire Cabochon

Wire Cutter

6 1-inch Silver-tone Eye Pins

6 1$^3/_4$-inch Silver-tone Head Pins

 12 4mm Faceted Acrylic Sapphire Beads

 2 8mm Faceted Acrylic Sapphire Beads

 6 6mm Faceted Acrylic Sapphire Beads

Needlenose Pliers

 4 9 × 8mm Antiqued Silver Mushroom Beads

 2 18mm Round Faceted Acrylic Sapphire Stones

Earring Backs with Posts or Clips

MAKING THE BARRETTE

1. Using the scissors, cut four 5-inch pieces and one 6-inch piece of black rattail cord.

2. Using the jewelry glue, glue one end of each of the five pieces of rattail cord to the top surface of the silver-tone barrette, as follows: the 6-inch piece in the center, one 5-inch piece $^1/_2$ inch in from each end, and one 5-inch piece halfway between the center piece and each outside piece.

3. Glue the 4-inch length of black satin ribbon centered across the top of the barrette so that it covers the rattail cord pieces. Fold the ends of the ribbon around to the back of the barrette and glue them in place. Trim the ends with the scissors.

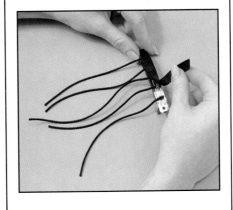

4. Tie a double overhand knot in each piece of rattail cord so that the top of the knot is $^1/_2$ inch below the barrette (see discussion of knots in "Techniques" section of Introduction).

5. String the beads onto the rattail pieces as follows: center piece—one 10mm antiqued silver melon bead, one 10.5mm corrugated antiqued silver disc, one 9 × 6mm barrel-shaped black pony bead, one 10.5mm corrugated antiqued silver disc, one 10mm antiqued silver melon bead; end pieces—one 9 × 6mm barrel-shaped black pony bead, one 10.5mm corrugated antiqued silver disc, one 10mm antiqued silver melon bead; remaining pieces—one 10.5mm corrugated antiqued silver disc, one 9 × 6mm barrel-shaped sapphire pony bead, one 10.5mm corrugated antiqued silver disc, one 10mm antiqued silver melon bead.

6. Tie a double overhand knot on each rattail cord piece to hold the beads. Trim the end of each cord piece with the scissors.

7. Glue three stone holders to the front of the barrette—the two oval ones at each end and a round one at the center. Glue the oval faceted acrylic sapphire stones and round acrylic sapphire cabochon to the holders.

MAKING THE EARRINGS

1. With the wire cutter, trim three silver-tone eye pins to measure $5/8$ inch. Glue the eye pins, separated from each other by about $1/8$ inch, to the back of a round stone holder.

2. Begin stringing beads on the three silver-tone head pins. Onto one head pin, which will be attached to the central eye pin of the earring, string one 4mm faceted acrylic sapphire bead, one 10mm antiqued silver melon bead, one 10.5mm corrugated antiqued silver disc, one 8mm faceted acrylic sapphire bead, one 6mm faceted

acrylic sapphire bead, one 4mm faceted acrylic sapphire bead. With the wire cutter, trim the head pin so that $1/4$ inch of wire extends beyond the beads. Using the needlenose pliers, bend the end of the pin to form a hook. Pass the hook through the central eye pin glued to the holder. Close the hook with the pliers.

3. Onto each of two other head pins, which will be attached to the remaining eye pins of the earring, string one 4mm faceted acrylic sapphire bead, one 9×8mm antiqued silver mushroom bead, one 6mm faceted acrylic sapphire bead, one 4mm faceted acrylic sapphire bead. As in step 2, trim the head pins and attach them to the eye pins on the stone holder.

4. Glue a round faceted acrylic sapphire to the stone holder. Glue on an earring back. Repeat for the second earring.

VARNISHED PAPER SLIDE/BUCKLE, PIN, AND EARRINGS

The bold, black-and-white design in this paper jewelry ensemble was inspired by Native American pottery designs of the Southwest. Embellished with inexpensive snake and lizard studs, the three pieces are a perfect complement to casual apparel with a Southwest flair.

8 × 10-inch Piece of Heat-bonding Material (we used Heat 'n' Bond heat-bonding material)

Iron

5-inch Square of Mat Board

2-inch Square of Poster Board

Permanent Black Marking Pen

Craft Knife

Scissors

1 Lizard-shaped Metal Stud

3 Snake-shaped Metal Studs

Wire Cutter

Black Acrylic Paint

Small Dish

No. 8 Flat Paintbrush

Waxed Paper

Toothbrush

Butter Knife

Water-based Matte Varnish

Varnish Brush

Jewelry Glue (we used Bond Victory 1991 glue)

Tweezers

1 Small Round Black Bead

Earring Backs with Posts

1-inch Pin Back

☉ ☉ ☉ ☉ ☉ ☉

1. Photocopy the design and feathers on the facing page. Following the manufacturer's directions, use the iron to apply the heat-bonding material to the back of the photocopy. Remove the paper backing and adhere the design to the mat board, the feathers to the poster board.

2. On the mat board, use the black marking pen to mark two 1 1/2-inch squares for earrings, one 1 3/4-inch square for the pin, and one 2 1/2 × 4-inch rectangle for the slide/buckle. Mark two 2 × 1/4-inch slits in the slide/buckle. Use the craft knife to cut out the pieces; cut out the feathers with the scissors.

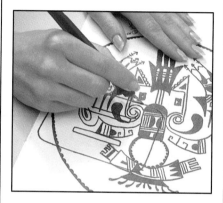

3. Cut the prongs from the backs of the lizard-shaped metal stud and the snake-shaped metal studs with the wire cutter.

4. Pour a small amount of the black acrylic paint into the small dish and dampen the No. 8 flat paintbrush. Touch the corner of the brush in the paint and blend the paint by brushing back and forth on the waxed paper. Brushing with short outward strokes, paint the edges of the *surface* of all the pieces, including the slide/buckle slits.

5. Dampen the toothbrush and dip it into the paint. Holding the brush close to the pieces, pull the butter knife across the bristles to spatter the paint onto the pieces.

6. When the paint is dry, apply a thin coat of the water-based matte varnish with the varnish brush to the decorated portion of each piece. Allow the varnish to dry.

7. With the jewelry glue, glue a snake-shaped metal stud to the center of each earring square. Glue the remaining snake-shaped metal stud to a corner of the slide/buckle.

8. Glue the feathers and the lizard-shaped metal stud to the pin square. Place a drop of jewelry glue near the lizard stud's back. Using the tweezers, place the small round black bead on the adhesive.

9. Glue an earring back to the top corner of the reverse side of an earring square, positioning it so

that the snake-shaped metal stud will appear upright when the earring is worn. Repeat for the other earring square.

10. Glue the pin back to the top corner of the pin square.

OLD WEST

FAUX TURQUOISE BUTTON COVERS

The faux turquoise gem stones in these casual but sophisticated button covers look so natural, only you will know they aren't real. The beauty of stone holders is that they also can be used to make post or clip back earrings. What a wonderful ensemble look you can create!

MATERIALS

 Jewelry Glue

 6 Silver-tone Button Cover Blanks

 6 Silver-tone Stone Holders

 6 Faux Turquoise Stones

⊙ ⊙ ⊙ ⊙ ⊙ ⊙

1. Using the jewelry glue, glue the back of a silver-tone button cover blank to the back of a silver-tone stone holder. Repeat with the remaining button cover blanks and stone holders.

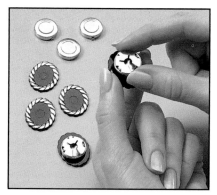

2. Glue a faux turquoise stone to a stone holder, positioning the stone inside the decorated edge of the holder. Repeat with the remaining stones.

VARIATIONS

Use your imagination! You can glue many kinds of stones to button cover backs, creating your own look, like the button covers shown with chevrons on black. To make earrings, simply use earring backs instead of button cover blanks.

DO - SI - DO

VARNISHED PAPER BOLO AND EARRINGS

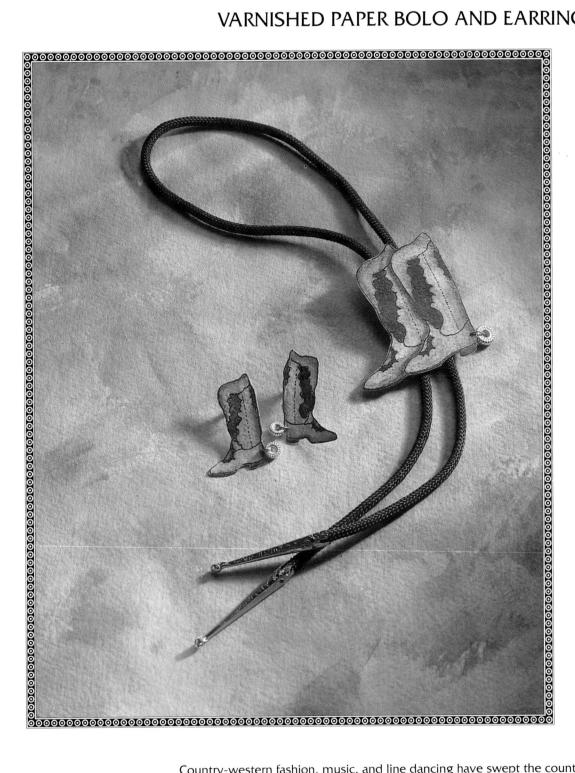

Country-western fashion, music, and line dancing have swept the country. With this bolo-and-earring ensemble, you're right in step with the new fad. Amazingly easy to make, the pieces will be finished before you can say "do-si-do"!

M A T E R I A L S

Tracing Paper

Thin-lead Pencil

4 × 5-inch Piece of 140-lb. Watercolor Paper

Fine-point Black Pen (made specifically for watercoloring)

Scissors

Red-brown Watercolor Pencil

Chocolate-brown Watercolor Pencil

No. 8 Angle Paintbrush

Jewelry Varnish (we used Jewelry Glaze jewelry varnish)

Varnish Brush

Small Nail

1 8mm Silver-tone Jump Ring

Needlenose Pliers

1 10.5mm Corrugated Silver-tone Disc

2 6mm Silver-tone Jump Rings

2 8mm Corrugated Silver-tone Discs

Jewelry Glue (we used Bond Victory 1991 glue)

Bolo Slide

Brown Bolo Cord

2 Silver-tone Bolo Tips

Earring Backs with Posts or Clips

☉ ☉ ☉ ☉ ☉ ☉

1. Place the tracing paper over the boot patterns on the facing page and trace the designs with the thin-lead pencil. Lay the tracing face down on the 140-lb. watercolor paper. Rub over the pencil marks with your thumbnail to transfer the marks to the watercolor paper.

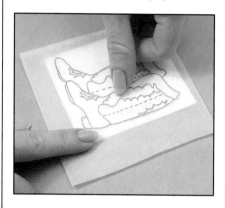

2. Remove the tracing paper and ink all the lines with the fine-point black pen. Cut out the pieces with the scissors.

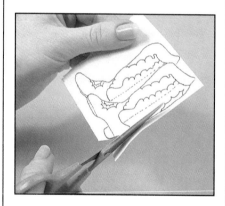

3. Using the side, not the point, of the red-brown watercolor pencil, color the entire surface of the bolo and earring pieces. Use the side of the chocolate-brown watercolor

pencil to shade the contours of the boots.

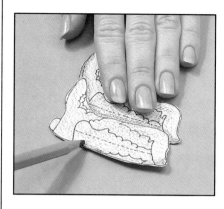

4. Use the point of the chocolate-brown pencil to color in the boot designs and heels.

5. Dampen the No. 8 angle paintbrush with water and brush over all areas except the brown designs in the boots and heels. Let the three pieces dry.

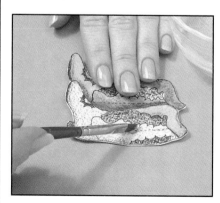

6. Wet the paintbrush again and use the point to dampen the brown designs and heels. Let them dry.

7. Apply a thin coat of jewelry varnish to the three pieces, using the varnish brush. Let them dry. Apply a second coat and let dry.

8. To place "spurs" on the boots for the three pieces, use the small nail to poke a hole at the back of each boot. For the bolo, open the 8mm silver-tone jump ring with the needlenose pliers and slip the 10.5mm corrugated silver-tone disc onto the ring. Insert the ring into the hole at the back of the pair of boots and close the ring with the pliers. Repeat for the earrings with the two 6mm silver-tone jump rings and the two 8mm corrugated silver-tone discs.

9. Using the jewelry glue, glue the bolo slide to the center back of the pair of boots. Thread the brown bolo cord through the slide. To attach the two silver-tone bolo tips, place glue on the ends of the cord and slip on the tips.

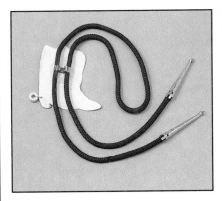

10. Glue the earring backs to the tops of the individual boots.

Bolo Pattern

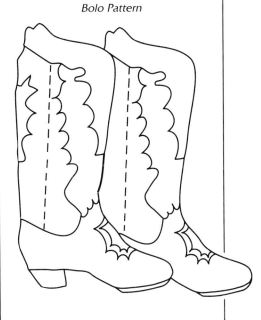

Earring Pattern

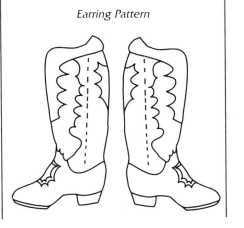

H O P I

TURQUOISE-AND-SILVER NECKLACE AND EARRINGS

The bright clarity of the desert Southwest is reflected in the simplicity of this Native-American-inspired design. No matter what you wear with this turquoise-and-silver ensemble, you'll be adding drama, interest—and an understated elegance.

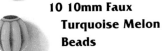
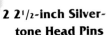

Needlenose Pliers

18-inch Length of 18-gauge Silver-tone Wire

33 19 × 6mm Oblong Silver-tone Beads

10 25 × 11mm Faux Turquoise Pony Beads

Wire Cutter

68-inch Length of 28-gauge Silver-tone Wire

8 3mm Round Silver-tone Beads

8 6mm Silver-tone Rondelles

14 10.5mm Corrugated Faux Turquoise Discs

10 10mm Faux Turquoise Melon Beads

2 2¹/₂-inch Silver-tone Head Pins

2 8mm Round Silver-tone Beads

2 10mm Silver-tone Discs

Silver-tone Earring Hooks

☉ ☉ ☉ ☉ ☉ ☉

MAKING THE NECKLACE

1. With the needlenose pliers, form a ¹/₄-inch hook in one end of the 18-gauge wire. At the other end, thread 11 19 × 6mm oblong silver-tone beads and all 10 25 × 11mm faux turquoise pony beads, alternating beads and starting and ending with an oblong silver-tone bead.

2. With the needlenose pliers, form a ¹/₄-inch hook in the other end of the wire. Hook the two ends together and bend the wire to form a circle.

3. With the wire cutter, cut the 28-gauge wire into eight pieces: two 12-inch pieces, two 10-inch pieces, two 8-inch pieces, and two 4-inch pieces.

4. Begin threading each of the eight pieces, starting with a 3mm silver-tone bead placed at the center of the wire. Twist the wire above the bead. You will be threading the remaining beads on two strands of wire, so that the silver bead is at the bottom.

5. Atop the 3mm silver bead on each 12-inch wire, thread one silver-tone rondelle, one corrugated faux turquoise disc, one oblong silver bead, one faux turquoise melon bead, one oblong silver bead, one corrugated faux turquoise disc, one oblong silver bead, one faux

turquoise melon bead, one oblong silver bead.

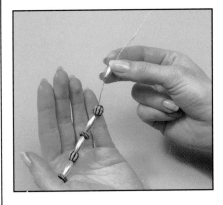

6. For each 10-inch wire, thread one silver rondelle atop the 3mm bead, then one faux turquoise corrugated disc, one oblong silver bead, one faux turquoise melon bead, one oblong silver bead, one corrugated faux turquoise disc, one oblong silver bead.

7. For each 8-inch wire, thread one silver rondelle atop the 3mm bead, then one faux turquoise corrugated disc, one oblong silver bead, one faux turquoise melon bead, one oblong silver bead.

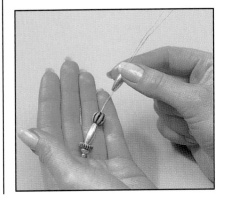

8. For each 4-inch wire, thread one silver rondelle atop the 3mm bead, then one corrugated faux turquoise disc and one oblong silver bead.

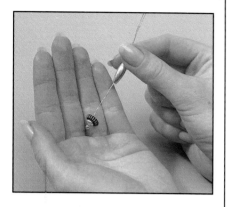

9. Attach the two 12-inch wires to the necklace, one on each side of the oblong silver bead at the center of the necklace circle, by wrapping the 28-gauge wire around the 18-gauge wire and twisting the thinner wire around itself several times. Trim any excess wire with the wire cutter.

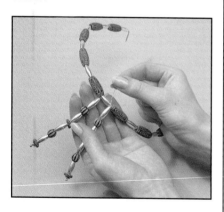

10. Attach the remaining wires to the necklace in descending lengths.

MAKING THE EARRINGS

1. Thread one head pin with one 8mm silver bead, one corrugated faux turquoise disc, one oblong silver bead, one faux turquoise melon bead, one silver disc.

2. With the pliers, form a loop in the end of the head pin and attach it to an earring hook. Close the loop. Repeat for the second earring.

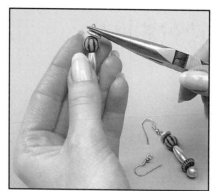

FABRIC NECKLACE AND EARRINGS

The beads used in the necklace may look difficult to make, but actually they're easily constructed, using grosgrain ribbon, heat-bonding material, and (yes!) paper clips. Use ribbon with a Navajo-inspired design and add to the ensemble by varying the motifs in the accompanying earrings.

M A T E R I A L S

Iron

21-inch Length of ⁷/₈-inch Heat-bonding Tape (we used Heat 'n' Bond heat-bonding tape)

21-inch Length of Grosgrain Ribbon (with repeating pattern)

Scissors

1 × 4-inch Piece of White Poster Board

Jewelry Glue (we used Bond Victory 1991 glue)

Toothpick

2 1-inch Silver-tone Eye Pins

Needlenose Pliers

Silver-tone Earring Hooks

50 Small Silver-tone Metal Paper Clips (of identical size and construction)

2 Dozen Clothespins

2 6mm Silver-tone Jump Rings

Silver-tone Necklace Clasp

⊙ ⊙ ⊙ ⊙ ⊙ ⊙

BEFORE YOU BEGIN

Iron the heat-bonding tape to the back of the grosgrain ribbon, following the manufacturer's directions. Leave the paper backing of the tape undisturbed.

MAKING THE EARRINGS

1. With the scissors, cut two pairs of matching designs from the grosgrain ribbon. Remove the paper backing from the heat-bonding tape and iron the pieces to the white poster board. Cut out the four squares.

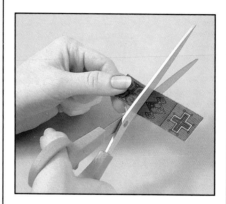

2. Using the jewelry glue applied with the toothpick, glue an eye pin diagonally to the back of an earring square so that the eye protrudes from the corner. Glue the second eye pin to the back of the matching square.

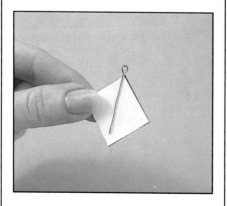

3. Glue the backs of the remaining two squares to the backs of the squares with eye pins so that each earring has a front side of one pattern and a back side of the other.

4. With the needlenose pliers, attach the earrings to the silver-tone earring hooks.

MAKING THE NECKLACE

1. Each *half*-bead of the necklace will consist of a ribbon envelope covering a silver-tone paper clip. To form the envelopes, cut 50 squares from the remaining grosgrain ribbon. Fold a square around a paper clip. Apply a thin line of jewelry glue near an edge of the square and cover with the opposite edge to form an envelope that fits the paper clip snugly.

2. Remove the paper clip. Secure the ribbon envelope with two clothespins until the glue is dry. Repeat with the remaining squares.

3. Begin assembling the necklace by hooking two paper clips to two other paper clips.

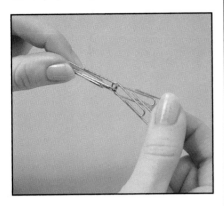

4. Slip a fabric envelope over one of the paper clips, seam side in. Slip a matching envelope on the opposite paper clip, seam side in. Repeat with the other pair of paper clips.

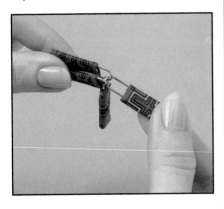

5. Attach two more paper clips to one of the already-covered pairs as in step 3; cover these with fabric envelopes as in step 4. Continue attaching paper clips and covering them with fabric envelopes until all 25 fabric beads are complete.

6. Using the pliers, open a 6mm silver-tone jump ring and attach it to the loop of one part of the necklace clasp and hook it around the two paper clips at one end of the necklace; close the ring. Repeat for the other part of the necklace clasp.

L A K O T A

FABRIC BARRETTE AND EARRINGS

This accessory ensemble—using patterned grosgrain ribbon inspired by
Lakota Sioux designs—simply couldn't be easier to make. Just heat-bond
your ribbon to poster board, glue on topaz and ruby acrylic stones, attach the
earring backs and barrette clamp, and you're ready to go!

M A T E R I A L S

Iron

24-inch Length of ³/₄-inch Heat-bonding Tape (we used Heat 'n' Bond heat-bonding tape)

12-inch Length of 1¹/₂-inch Grosgrain Ribbon

12-inch Length of 1¹/₂-inch-wide Poster Board

Scissors

Jewelry Glue (we used Bond Victory 1991 glue)

Tweezers

 2 7mm Round Faceted Acrylic Topazes

Earring Backs with Posts or Clips

Ruler

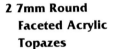 **1 22 × 10mm Diamond-shaped Faceted Acrylic Ruby**

2 5mm Round Faceted Acrylic Topazes

1 3-inch Barrette Clamp

2 or 3 Clothespins

◉ ◉ ◉ ◉ ◉ ◉

BEFORE YOU BEGIN

Iron the heat-bonding tape to the wrong side of the grosgrain ribbon, following the manufacturer's directions. Remove the paper backing and iron the ribbon to the poster board.

MAKING THE EARRINGS

1. Using the scissors, carefully cut out two matching design sections from the ribbon.

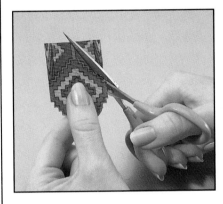

2. Using the jewelry glue and tweezers, glue a 7mm round faceted acrylic topaz to the center of an earring. Glue an earring back to the top corner of the back side of the earring. Repeat for the second earring.

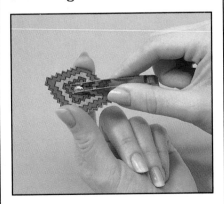

MAKING THE BARRETTE

1. Using the ruler and scissors, carefully cut out a 4-inch design section from the ribbon. Glue the 22 × 10mm diamond-shaped faceted acrylic ruby to the center, then glue the two 5mm round faceted acrylic topazes to each side of the center stone.

2. Glue the barrette clamp to the center of the back of the barrette. Secure it with two or three clothespins until the glue is dry.

ARIA

PEARL NECKLACE AND BRACELET

For that special occasion when only pearls will do, this sophisticated necklace-and-bracelet duo will add a soft splendor to your cocktail or formal apparel. What's special about the design is the detachable shell decorated with black pearls, lending natural beauty to this incomparable ensemble.

M A T E R I A L S

- **Beading Needle**
- **White Nylon Beading Thread**
- **4 Gold Bead Tips**
- **Toothpick**
- **Jewelry Glue**
- **Beading Board**
- **67 8mm White Pearls**
- **16 4mm Gold Beads**
- **15 6mm Black Pearls**
- **Tweezers**
- **9mm Gold-tone Spring Ring Clasp**
- **Needlenose Pliers**
- **18 6mm White Pearls**
- **7mm Gold-tone Spring Ring Clasp**
- **Wire Cutter**
- **Shell-shaped Gold French Ear Clip**
- **Decorative Half-shell**
- **4- to 5-inch Length of Gold Jewelry Wire**
- **20 2mm Black Pearls**

⊙ ⊙ ⊙ ⊙ ⊙ ⊙

MAKING THE NECKLACE

1. Thread the beading needle with a single strand of white nylon beading thread; tie one or two overhand knots in one end, depending on the thread's thickness (see discussion of knots in "Techniques" section of Introduction).

2. Slide the needle through a bead tip, entering from the top down; your knot should sit inside the cup. Tie an overhand knot on the other side of the bead tip and, with the toothpick, place a dab of jewelry glue in the bead tip cup to hold the knot in place.

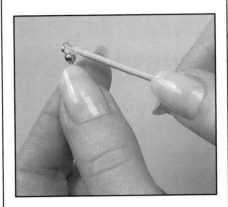

3. Lay your bead design on the beading board in the following pattern: 15 8mm white pearls, one 4mm gold bead, one 6mm black pearl, one 4mm gold bead, 16 8mm white pearls, one 4mm gold bead, one 6mm black pearl, one 4mm gold bead, five 8mm white pearls, one 4mm gold bead, one 6mm black pearl, one 4mm gold bead, 16 8mm white pearls, one 4mm gold bead, one 6mm black pearl, one 4mm gold bead, 15 8mm white pearls. String on the beads in that order.

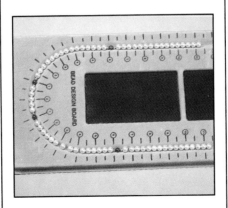

4. String on a second bead tip. Make a loose overhand knot, using the tweezers to slide the knot close to the bead tip. Guide the thread

until it is in place, then tighten it at the bead tip.

5. Hook the bead tips to the 9mm gold-tone spring ring clasp and close them, using the needlenose pliers.

MAKING THE BRACELET

1. Thread the beading needle with a single thread and attach a gold bead tip the same way you did with the pearl necklace.

2. Lay out your bead design on the beading board in the following pattern: three 6mm white pearls, one 4mm gold bead, one 6mm black pearl, one 4mm gold bead, four 6mm white pearls, one 4mm gold bead, one 6mm black pearl, one 4mm gold bead, four 6mm white pearls, one 4mm gold bead, one 6mm black pearl, one 4mm gold bead, four 6mm white pearls, one 4mm gold bead, one 6mm black pearl, one 4mm gold bead, three 6mm white pearls. String on the beads in that order.

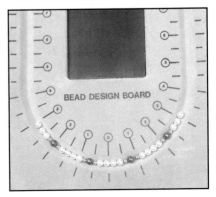

3. Attach the final bead tip the same way as with the necklace.

4. Hook the bead tips to the 7mm gold-tone spring ring clasp and close them, using the pliers.

MAKING THE PENDANT

1. Using the wire cutter, remove the stem from the shell-shaped gold French ear clip.

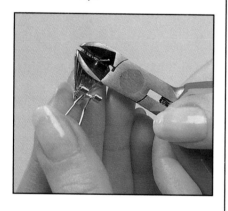

2. Attach the ear clip to the decorative half-shell using the gold jewelry wire strung through a hole near the top of the shell (the hole may either be naturally occurring or be drilled by hand). Clip off any excess wire, then glue the wire to the back of the shell.

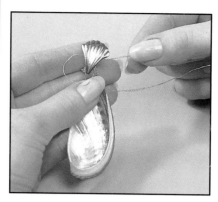

3. Using the tweezers to place them, glue the 20 2mm black pearls and remaining 6mm black pearls to the inside of the shell and let dry.

4. Place the shell pendant on the necklace.

VICTORIANA

This charming reproduction of porcelain pins from the turn of the century will make a wonderful addition to your jewelry collection. The hard part is choosing the print you want for the porcelain oval. But, since the piece is so easy to make, why not create several variations?

MATERIALS

Scissors

Victorian Color Print

1¹/₂-inch Porcelain Oval

White Glue

Small Bowl or Cup

Small Brush (for glue)

2 Small Sponges

Jewelry Glue

Toothpick

2-inch Jewelry Setting

Waxed Paper

2-part Polymer Finish

Brush (for polymer finish)

1-inch Pin Back

◎ ◎ ◎ ◎ ◎ ◎

1. With the scissors, cut out your Victorian color print to fit the porcelain oval.

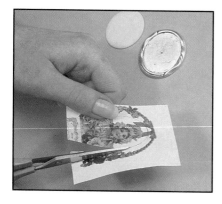

2. Mix three parts white glue to one part water in the small bowl or cup. With the small brush, apply the glue sparingly to the surface of the oval (any excess will cause the design to pucker).

3. Place the cutout on the oval. Dip a finger in the glue and spread the glue thinly and evenly over the cutout area.

4. Dampen one of the small sponges and use it to press the cutout into place on the oval, squeezing out air bubbles and excess glue. Start at the middle of the cutout and work outward. Dampen your fingers and continue to massage the cutout until it is free of all bubbles and has fully adhered to the surface. You will have about a minute before the glue sets up. Allow a few minutes after this, then clean up around the design with the second small

sponge dipped in water. Let the oval dry overnight.

5. Using the jewelry glue and toothpick, glue the oval to the jewelry setting.

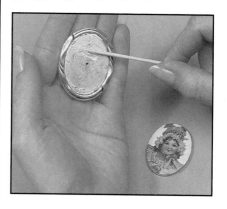

6. Place the piece on the waxed paper. Following the manufacturer's directions, mix the two-part polymer finish. Using the second brush, apply a thin coat to the piece. Let it dry four hours. Apply a second coat and let it dry overnight.

7. Glue on the pin back, using the jewelry glue and toothpick.

VARIATIONS

Just about any small-size Victorian color print, like the lady with flowers and the beribboned cat shown on the previous page, can be used to make this charming, vintage-look porcelain ornament.

VINTAGE

BEADED STICKPIN AND EARRINGS

Come back to turn-of-the-century elegance with this romantic jewelry ensemble. Variety is the key: Different sizes and shapes of beads stacked just the right way give the desired effect. The perfect complement to contemporary fashions—or those vintage resale finds!

M A T E R I A L S

1 12mm Round Black Acrylic Bead

1 5-inch Gold-tone Stickpin

Jewelry Glue (we used Bond Victory 1991 glue)

Toothpick

10 10mm Gold-tone Discs

3 Ornamental Antiqued Gold Pony Beads

1 Ornamental Gold-tone Pony Bead

3 10mm Gold-tone Melon Beads

3 12 × 8mm Oval Gold-tone Beads

2 6mm Round Gold-tone Beads

1 Gold-tone Clutch (for stickpin)

2 3mm Round Gold-tone Beads

2 8-inch Lengths of 28-gauge Gold Wire

2 4mm Round Black Acrylic Beads

Gold-tone Earring Hooks

Wire Cutter

MAKING THE STICKPIN

1. Glue the 12mm round black acrylic bead to the top of the gold-tone stickpin, using the jewelry glue and the toothpick.

2. Thread your beads onto the stickpin, securing them with a dot of jewelry glue applied with the toothpick between the beads, in this order: one 10mm gold-tone disc, one ornamental antiqued gold pony bead, one 10mm gold-tone disc, one ornamental gold-tone pony bead, one 10mm gold-tone disc, one 10mm gold-tone melon bead, one 10mm gold-tone disc, and one 12 × 8mm oval gold-tone bead, followed by the gold-tone clutch.

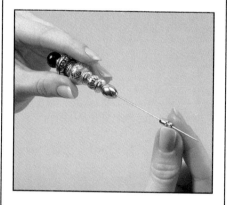

MAKING THE EARRINGS

1. Thread one 3mm round gold-tone bead at the center of an 8-inch length of 28-gauge gold wire. Twist the wire to hold the bead in place.

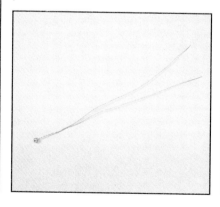

2. Thread the remaining beads over two strands of wire, on top of the 3mm round gold-tone bead, in this order: one 4mm round black acrylic bead, one 10mm gold-tone disc, one ornamental antiqued gold pony bead, one 10mm gold-tone disc, one 10mm gold-tone melon bead, one 10mm gold-tone disc, one 12 × 8mm oval gold-tone bead, one 6mm round gold-tone bead.

3. Thread the two strands of wire through the loop of a gold-tone earring hook. Twist the wire around itself several times and trim any excess with the wire cutter. Repeat for the second earring.

LEGACY

ONYX-LOOK PIN

Onyx-like faceted acrylic stones and decorative gold chains adorn a gold-filigreed back in this delightful reproduction of vintage pins. Perfect for suit jackets and heavy sweaters, Legacy will become one of your favorite pieces of jewelry, as attractive and versatile as it is timeless.

Jewelry Glue

60mm Filigreed Gold-tone Pin Back (we used an American Art Clay Company pin back)

2 10mm Round Black Faceted Acrylic Stones

1 15mm Octagonal Black Faceted Acrylic Stone

Toothpick

8-inch Gold-tone Chain

Wire Cutter

Tweezers

5 7mm Round Black Faceted Acrylic Stones

1. Place a generous amount of jewelry glue at the center of the filigreed gold-tone pin back and set in the two 10mm round black faceted and one 15mm octagonal black faceted acrylic stones. Let the glue dry.

2. Using the toothpick, place a small amount of jewelry glue around the round stone on your left. Beginning at the top of this

stone, wrap the gold-tone chain counterclockwise. Place glue across the top of the central octagonal stone, then bring the chain across it.

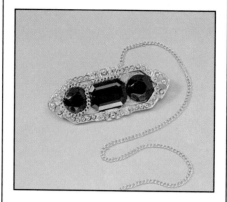

3. Place glue around the stone on your right and wrap the chain counterclockwise around it.

4. Place glue along the sides and bottom of the central octagonal stone, then bring the chain down, across the bottom, and up the left side to where you began wrapping. Let dry. Trim the chain with the wire cutter.

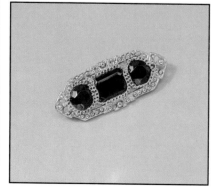

5. With the wire cutter, cut off a 2-inch length and a 2¹/₂-inch length from the chain. Glue on each as a loop beneath the central octagonal stone.

6. Using the tweezers to place them, glue on the five 7mm round black faceted acrylic stones, four at the corners around the central octagonal stone and one at the center top of the pin back.

TIMELY

WATCH PARTS COLLAGE PIN AND EARRINGS

Just about every home has one or two wristwatches that are beyond repair.
Use them to make this fashionable pin-and-earring duo! Add loose watch
parts from your local craft store, glue on odd pieces of old jewelry,
and you have a unique ensemble.

Jewelry Glue

3-inch Metal or Wooden Disc

2 Packages Each of Watch Parts (available in most craft stores)

Old Watches (from home)

Old Costume Jewelry Pearls, Beads, and Stones

1¹/₂-inch Pin Back

Toothpick

1-inch Earring Clip Back Discs

8-inch Gold-tone Chain

Wire Cutter

☉ ☉ ☉ ☉ ☉ ☉

MAKING THE PIN

Assortment of smaller watch parts

1. Apply a liberal amount of jewelry glue to the 3-inch metal or wooden disc.

2. Selecting from the packaged watch parts, set in a couple of large pieces, such as the watch face shown.

3. Gently sprinkle smaller watch pieces around and on top of the large pieces, in whatever design you want, and let dry. Apply jewelry glue to the areas that need to be built up. Add to your design with old watches from home.

Sprinkle on ornamental pearls, beads, and stones from old costume jewelry.

4. Glue on the pin back, using the toothpick to apply the jewelry glue.

MAKING THE EARRINGS

1. Place a liberal amount of jewelry glue on one earring clip back disc.

2. Cut two 2-inch pieces from the 8-inch gold-tone chain, using the wire cutter. Make them into loops and place the pieces on the glue at the bottom center of the earring.

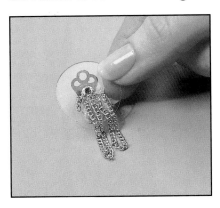

3. Glue two large watch parts on top of the chain loops.

4. Apply glue to the surface of the large watch parts and sprinkle on smaller watch parts. Build up your design, covering part of the larger pieces. Repeat for the second earring.

AUTUMN GOLD

GOLD-LEAF-BEAD NECKLACE AND EARRINGS

Cascades of shimmering gold will add festive flair to your party outfit. Gold-colored thread and assorted gold-tone leaf charms combine to create a rich tangle of color and shine.

M A T E R I A L S

Ruler

Scissors

11-yard Length of Gold-colored Thread (we used Madeira Glisten Gloss Sparkle thread)

Jewelry Glue (we used Bond Victory 1991 glue)

105 Assorted Small Gold-tone Leaf Beads

1 Large-hole Gold-tone Necklace Clasp (hooked)

2 6-inch Lengths of 24-gauge Gold-tone Wire

Wire Cutter

2 6mm Gold-tone Jump Rings

Needlenose Pliers

Gold-tone Earring Hooks

⊙ ⊙ ⊙ ⊙ ⊙ ⊙ ⊙

MAKING THE NECKLACE

1. Using the ruler and scissors, cut the gold-colored thread into 11 36-inch pieces. Tie an overhand knot in one end of each piece (see discussion of knots in "Techniques" section of Introduction). Apply a small amount of jewelry glue to the other end of each piece to prevent fraying. Let the glue dry.

2. Thread one gold-tone leaf bead onto the glued end of a strand of gold-colored thread and place it about 7 inches from the knot. Secure the leaf bead in that position by tying an overhand knot in the thread. Place eight more leaf beads on the strand about 2 inches apart, securing each with an overhand knot. Repeat with the remaining 10 strands of gold-colored thread.

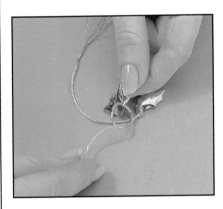

3. For one side of the necklace, gather the ends of all 11 strands and put them through the hole of one hook of the gold-tone necklace clasp. Apply jewelry glue to the ends of the strands after they have been wrapped around the clasp hole.

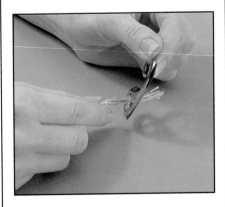

4. Before the jewelry glue dries, wrap the looped strands tightly with a 6-inch length of the 24-gauge gold-tone wire. Trim any excess wire with the wire cutter.

When the jewelry glue has dried, trim any excess thread with the scissors. Repeat steps 3 and 4 with the opposite ends of the strands and the other part of the necklace clasp.

MAKING THE EARRINGS

1. Open a 6mm gold-tone jump ring with the needlenose pliers. Place three leaf beads of different designs onto the jump ring.

2. Attach the jump ring to the loop of a gold-tone earring hook. Close the ring with the pliers. Repeat for the second earring.

S E A S H O R E

MOLDED PLASTIC EARRINGS

Who would guess that you didn't buy these charming shell-shaped earrings at a boutique or department store? Working with plastic modeling material is probably one of the easiest skills to get the hang of—and if you make a mistake, just rewarm the plastic and recast it in your shell molds.

MATERIALS

3 × 1½-inch Piece of Iridescent Plastic Modeling Material (we used Friendly Plastic plastic modeling material)

Shell-shaped Metal Earring Molds (right and left)

Nonaluminum, Heat-resistant Mixing Bowl

Scissors

Toothpick

Jewelry Glue

Earring Backs

⊙ ⊙ ⊙ ⊙ ⊙ ⊙

See also "Techniques" section of Introduction.

1. Cut your iridescent plastic modeling material slightly larger than the shell-shaped metal molds.

2. Fill the nonaluminum, heat-resistant mixing bowl with water heated to 140-150 degrees Fahrenheit. Soften the plastic in the water and press it into both molds.

3. After the plastic has hardened, remove it from the molds and trim the excess with the scissors. Soften the pieces in warm water again to smooth out any rough edges.

4. Using the toothpick to apply the jewelry glue, attach the earring backs to the shells.

BIJOUX

PLASTIC PIN

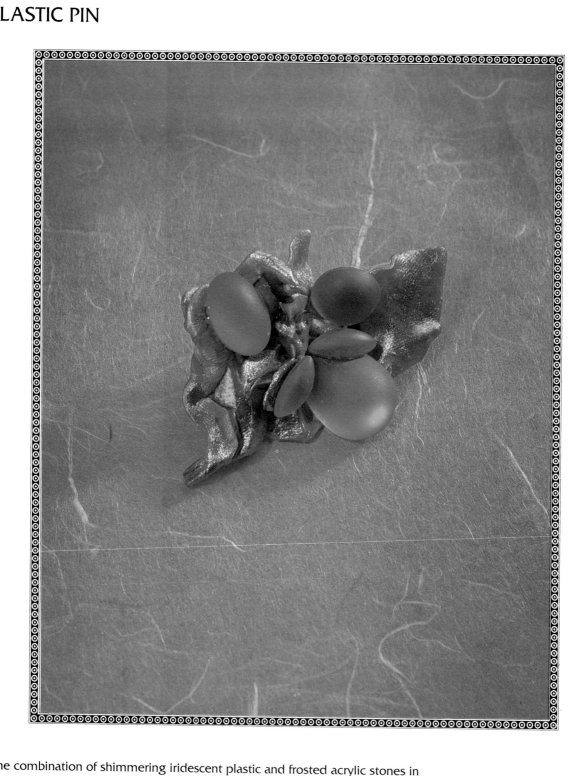

The combination of shimmering iridescent plastic and frosted acrylic stones in turquoise-green and magenta makes for a delightful—and delightfully quirky—design. Each time you fashion your plastic modeling material by hand, you create a unique piece. Let your imagination be your guide!

Nonaluminum, Heat-resistant Mixing Bowl

3 × 1½-inch Piece of Iridescent Turquoise Plastic Modeling Material (we used Friendly Plastic plastic modeling material)

3 × 1½-inch Piece of Magenta-silver Plastic Modeling Material (we used Friendly Plastic plastic modeling material)

Scissors

1 25 × 18mm Frosted Turquoise Teardrop

1 18 × 13mm Oval Frosted Magenta Cabochon

1 16mm Round Frosted Turquoise Cabochon

Jewelry Glue

2 12 × 7mm Frosted Magenta Navettes

1-inch Pin Back

⊙　⊙　⊙　⊙　⊙　⊙

See also "Techniques" section of Introduction.

1. Fill the nonaluminum, heat-resistant mixing bowl with water heated to 140-150 degrees Fahrenheit. Soften the piece of iridescent turquoise plastic modeling material in the water until it is pliable. Scrunch the piece into a pleasing shape.

2. From the piece of magenta-silver plastic modeling material, use the scissors to cut four pieces measuring ¼ inch by the width of the plastic. Soften the pieces in the warm water, then place them in the center and on one side of the turquoise plastic, working them into the piece. If the plastic hardens, dip it in warm water to soften and shape it.

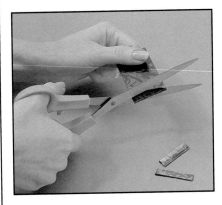

3. Glue on the frosted turquoise teardrop, oval frosted magenta cabochon, and round frosted turquoise cabochon, using the jewelry glue.

4. When the adhesive dries, glue on the frosted magenta navettes, one on each side of the narrow end of the teardrop.

5. Glue on the pin back.

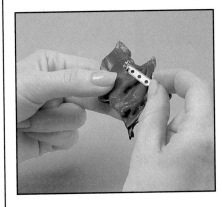

CELEBRATION

MARBLED PAPER PIN AND EARRINGS

It's hard to believe jewelry that looks so sophisticated could actually be made
of wrapping paper and glue—but it is! High-quality paper, of course, makes
all the difference, giving the pieces the look of metal and stone. The clear
polymer coating provides a beautifully deep luster.

MATERIALS

Scissors

1 Sheet of Marbled Gift Wrapping or Hand-marbled Paper

1 Sheet of Blue Origami-type Metallic Paper

White Glue

Small Bowl or Cup

Small Brush (for glue)

Toothpick

Scissors

Waxed Paper

2-part Polymer Finish

Brush (for polymer finish)

1¹/₂-inch Pin Back

Earring Backs

◉ ◉ ◉ ◉ ◉ ◉

1. With the scissors, cut eight strips of marbled paper and eight strips of blue origami-type metallic paper, each 3 inches by 1¹/₄ inches.

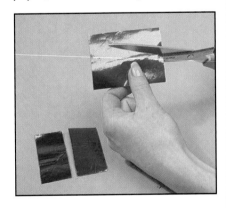

2. Mix three parts white glue to one part water in the small bowl or cup. Glue the metallic strips to the marbled strips, wrong side to wrong side, applying the glue with the small brush. Trim the edges if needed. Let dry.

3. For one side of the pin, fold two of the eight glued strips in half widthwise. Slip one strip inside the other, metallic blue side facing marbled side. This results in four flaps of paper.

4. On a level surface, place the folded end toward you and pick up the right corner of the first (top) flap. Fold it back, leaving ¹/₂ inch of the marbled paper showing.

Fold back the right corner of the next three flaps, leaving ¹/₄ inch showing between each fold.

5. Using the white glue and the toothpick, glue the four layers to each other on the inside, leaving the folded flaps free.

6. Repeat this procedure to fashion the other half of the pin, *making sure that you create a mirror-image piece.* That's because you are constructing left and right halves of the pin.

7. Glue the two pin halves together at their folded ends, using the toothpick to apply the adhesive. Trace this new shape on a piece of marbled paper, cut the shape out with scissors, and glue it to the back of the pin.

8. For the earrings, repeat steps 3 through 6—with one change: In putting the already-glued strips together, *have metallic side facing metallic* before you fold the strips widthwise. (As you did for the pin, be sure to construct an earring piece *and its mirror image*—you're making right and left earrings.)

9. Place the pin and earring pieces on the waxed paper. Following the manufacturer's directions, mix the two-part polymer finish. Using the brush, apply a thin coat to the pieces. Let the pieces dry four hours, then apply a second coat and let dry overnight.

10. Glue on the pin back and earring backs.

S A N T A

PUZZLE PIN

Discarded puzzle pieces make for trendy costume jewelry. They're also great as stocking stuffers or smaller birthday gifts. The pins can be as simple or as elaborate as you wish; it all depends on how they're painted and decorated. Show off your artistic talent—and your whimsical side!

MATERIALS

Puzzle Piece

Thin-lead Pencil

Small Round Paintbrush

Acrylic Paint in Fleshtone, Red, White Pearl, and Black (we used DecoArt Americana acrylic flesh-tone, red, and black paints and Tulip Color Point Paint Stitching acrylic paint in ivory)

Waxed Paper

2-part Polymer Finish

Brush (for polymer finish)

1-inch Pin Back

Toothpick

Jewelry Glue

◎ ◎ ◎ ◎ ◎ ◎

1. Paint the puzzle piece with acrylic fleshtone paint, using the small round paintbrush. Let it dry. Apply a second coat.

2. With the thin-lead pencil, mark the hat line, eye, and mouth.

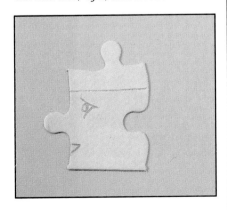

3. Paint the hat with acrylic red paint, applying two coats.

4. Build up acrylic white pearl paint on the hat band and hat tassel.

Draw lines with the acrylic white pearl paint for the beard, hair, and mustache. Let dry.

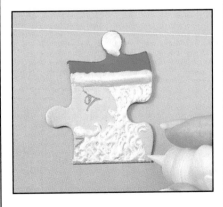

5. Paint the eye and lashes in acrylic black paint. Paint the mouth in acrylic red paint with an outline in acrylic black. After the black paint of the eye has dried, apply a small dot of acrylic white pearl paint as a highlight.

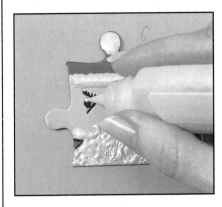

6. Place the puzzle piece on the waxed paper. Following the manufacturer's directions, mix the two-part polymer finish. Using the brush, apply a thin coat to the puzzle piece. Let it dry four hours. Apply a second coat and let it dry overnight.

7. Glue on the pin back, using the toothpick to apply the jewelry glue.

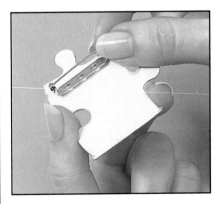

VARIATIONS

Put your drawing skills to use and create new faces for your puzzle pieces, like the lady and little boy's heads shown. Explore with different colors of paint, perhaps experiment by gluing on bits and pieces of old jewelry, like rhinestones and beads.

VISAGE

JEWELED PORCELAIN PIN

The stylized playfulness of Art Deco is captured in this jewel-encrusted porcelain pin, perfect as an accent for everything from daytime office attire to casual weekend apparel. Wear it in good style!

MATERIALS

Thin-lead Pencil

Three-quarter 2-inch Porcelain Face

Acrylic Paint in Metallic Gold, Iridescent Lavender, and Iridescent Pale Green (we used DecoArt Americana acrylic gold paint and Tulip Color Point Paint Stitching acrylic paint in lilac and celery)

Small Brush

Jewelry Glue

3 18×8mm Faceted Black Acrylic Teardrops

Tweezers

2 18×8mm Faceted Fuchsia Acrylic Teardrops

1 18×8mm Faceted Lavender Acrylic Teardrop

4 7mm Round Faceted Fuchsia Acrylic Stones

1-inch Pin Back

⊙ ⊙ ⊙ ⊙ ⊙ ⊙

1. Using the thin-lead pencil, divide the top of the three-quarter porcelain face into five sections.

2. Paint over the pencil lines with metallic gold acrylic paint, using the small brush.

3. Dot the sections on the side and in the center of the head with iridescent lavender acrylic paint.

4. Dot the sections in between with iridescent pale green acrylic paint. Let dry.

5. Place a generous amount of jewelry glue at the neck portion of the face. Glue the faceted black acrylic teardrops in place, gripping them with the tweezers.

6. Glue the faceted fuchsia acrylic teardrops in place, using the tweezers.

7. Glue the faceted lavender acrylic teardrop in place, using the tweezers.

8. Glue three round faceted fuchsia acrylic stones to the neck and one to the forehead, using the tweezers.

9. Glue on the pin back.

CONFETTI

SPARKLE-BEAD NECKLACE AND EARRINGS

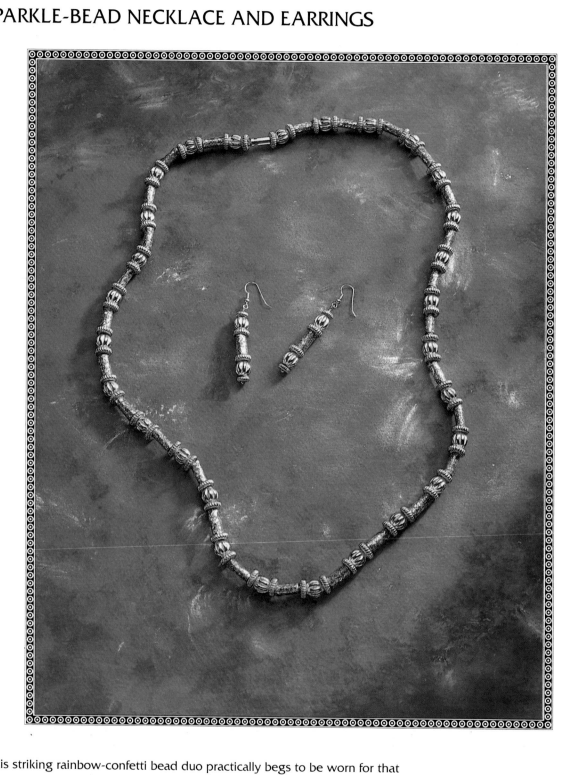

This striking rainbow-confetti bead duo practically begs to be worn for that special evening on the town. It may surprise you to find that the sparkle beads start as simple acrylic paint applied to plastic wrap. But, then, some of the loveliest things have the humblest beginnings!

MATERIALS

- **12 × 18-inch Cardboard**
- **12 × 20-inch Piece of Plastic Food Wrap**
- **Transparent Plastic Tape**
- **Sparkle Paint (we used Liquid Sequins sparkle paint)**
- **Butter Knife**
- **Ruler**
- **Craft Knife**
- **6 Narrow Drinking Straws**
- **Jewelry Glue (we used Bond Victory 1991 glue)**
- **Toothpick**
- **40-inch Length of Gold Rattail Cord**
- **Wire Cutter**
- **12-inch Length of 28-gauge Gold-tone Wire**
- **Gold-tone Necklace Clasp**
- **60 10.5mm Corrugated Gold-tone Discs**
- **32 10mm Gold-tone Melon Beads**
- **Scissors**
- **4 2mm Round Gold-tone Beads**
- **4 6mm Corrugated Gold-tone Discs**
- **Gold-tone Earring Hooks**

MAKING THE NECKLACE

1. Cover the cardboard with the plastic food wrap, securing the plastic at the back with the transparent plastic tape. Pour the sparkle paint over this surface to cover a 12 × 18-inch area, using the butter knife to smooth out the painted surface. Allow it to dry.

2. Remove the paint-covered plastic wrap from the cardboard. Using the ruler and craft knife, measure and cut 29 strips 2¹/₂ inches long and ¹/₂ inch wide.

3. To make the sparkle beads, roll the strips around the drinking straws to form ¹/₂-inch-wide cylinders of several layers, 29 cylinders in all. Secure each cylinder with a thin line of jewelry glue applied with the toothpick. Remove the sparkle beads from the straws when the adhesive is dry.

4. Make a small loop in one end of the gold rattail cord and secure it with glue. Using the wire cutter, cut a small piece from the 28-gauge gold-tone wire. Attach one part of the gold-tone necklace clasp to the rattail loop with the piece of wire.

5. String the beads on the rattail cord in the following order: one 10.5mm corrugated gold-tone disc, one 10mm gold-tone melon bead, one 10.5mm corrugated gold-tone disc, one sparkle bead. Repeat the pattern until you have used 27 of the sparkle beads. Finish with one 10.5mm corrugated gold-tone disc, one 10mm gold-tone

melon bead, one 10.5mm corrugated gold-tone disc.

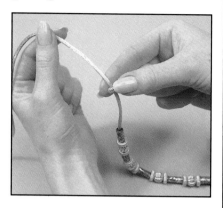

6. Trim any excess rattail cord with the scissors. Make a loop in the other end of the rattail cord, apply glue to secure it, and attach the other part of the necklace clasp, as in step 4. Trim with the scissors.

MAKING THE EARRINGS

1. Cut the remaining 28-gauge wire in half with the wire cutter. Place a 2mm round gold-tone bead on one wire, holding it in the center of the wire by twisting the wire above it. On top of the bead, thread one 6mm corrugated gold-tone disc on the double strand of wire, followed by one 10mm gold-tone melon bead, one 10.5mm corrugated gold-tone disc, one sparkle bead, one 10.5mm corrugated gold-tone disc, one 10mm gold-tone melon bead, one 6mm corrugated gold-tone disc, one 2mm round gold-tone bead.

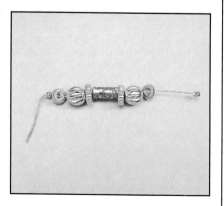

2. Insert the double strand of wire into the loop of a gold-tone earring hook. Twist the wire several times to secure it. Trim any excess wire with the wire cutter. Repeat for the second earring.

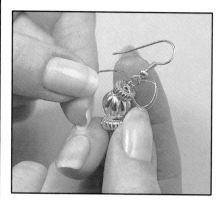